AF445607

Chapter Two - Free SVG Images Online

Another great thing about SVG cutting files is you can find many free ones online, ergo the reason I wrote this valuable guide. In Chapter Six, Where to Find Free SVG Files I've listed more than 150 sites where you can find free cut files for any cutting machine that uses SVG images.

You can also purchase bundles of SVG files that are cheaper than if you bought each file separately. They are usually themed bundles like kids, seasons, animals, weddings, and so many other choices. But with the unlimited free files listed in this book you may never have to buy another cut file for you die cutter.

What to expect when downloading files

To make sure the resources listed in this book where as valuable as I think they are I visited every single site verifying they offered free SVG files.

Before considering whether to add a website to my list I read every about me page I could find to learn more about these talented and generous designers.

Some sites you may be familiar with are not listed here. I purposely ignored database sites that are just a depository of digital files because they seemed cold and impersonal and were not run by real crafters like you and I. These include GeekSvg.com, Svgsilh.com, Lovesvg.com and Freesvg.org to name just a few. You may find these useful so I've listed them here.

Many craft bloggers share SVG files if you sign up for their email list which gives you access to their image library filled with free downloadable graphics.

While other sites allow you to download the file just by clicking on it. Still other sites require you to set up a free account to add the file to your shopping cart to download it.

The SVG file will be zipped and usually includes a DXF, SVG, PNG and EPS file. **Treat these files like you would any other download and scan them to keep your device secure.**

When you start collecting free Cricut images you may want to set up folders for types of themes. Try to be specific when naming your folders using subfolders to keep files organized.

Uploading a SVG file into Design Space

Downloaded SVG zip files are compressed and you'll need to extract the files before you can work with each individual image.

TIP: If you get a message saying "this file is unsupported" you probably tried to upload the .zip file into Design Space. Unzip the files first.

Open Design Space. From the homepage click on **New Project** which will bring up the canvas. From the canvas click on **Upload**. Then hit the **Upload Image** button which brings up a window. Drag or drop the file or browse and select the SVG file.

TIP: Your computer may not recognize SVG files. Look for your browser icon as the thumbnail of a SVG file or HTML document. Design Space will recognize it as a SVG file even in this format.

The uploaded image will appear. You can rename it if you choose and add tags to make it easier to find later in your library of saved images.

You can now find it in the **Recently Uploaded Images**. At that point you can select it and hit **Insert Images** into the canvas to start your project.

When you upload a SVG or DFX file into Design Space and they will upload as multiple layers with each element being separated into individual layers.

When you use files you find online make sure you check their terms of use. Some are for your personal use, and you may or may not sell the items you make unless you own the commercial license for the file. Some include a commercial license for free while others will sell you a license.

Once you start finding images online you may be tempted to sell items using cartoon characters and logos for professional sports teams but remember these items are copyrighted.

Using Cricut templates in Design Space

Once you have tons of cut files using Cricut templates can make the design process even easier. You can see how big or small the design needs to be to fit the actual item. Working with clothing is especially helpful since you can choose different sizes.

Choose from **Home Decor**, **Fashion** and **Kids Crafts** or any other category when designing with **Templates** in Design Space.

Seeing what the image looks like on a wine glass, backpack, tag, candle or banner is a great way to save material and avoid mistakes.

TIP: Remember when you hit the **Make It** button only the design will cut out not the template itself.

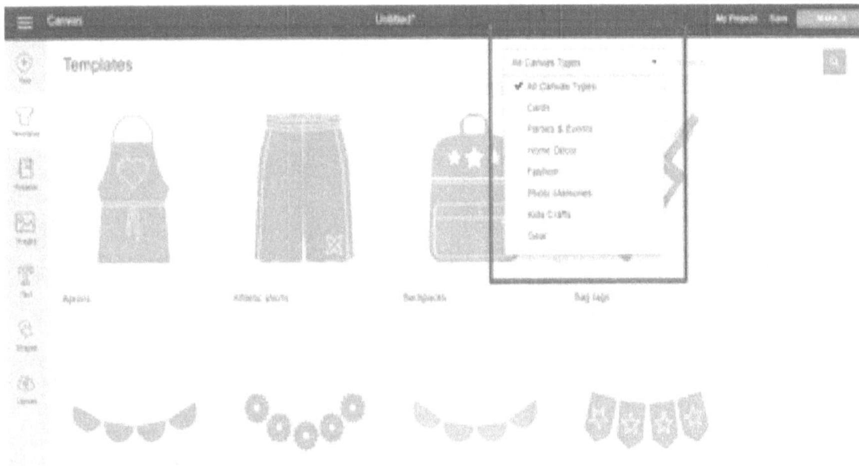

Chapter Three - Creating Your Own SVG Files

If you find an image you want to use but it's not a SVG file, it's easy to convert. Some images will convert better than others. When searching for images it's easiest to use clipart images or coloring pages. For instance, "mickey mouse clipart" or "mickey mouse coloring page".

Conversion software has to trace the uploaded image to map out or define the outline to be able to print or cut the defined area. For the best results look for images with high contrast between dark and light colors. An image with well-defined lines and not a lot of intricate detail will work best.

Converting other image file types to SVG files

Go to this website:

www.image.online-convert.com

Scroll down to "convert image to SVG format"

Use the "choose files" option

You can then make changes if you want such as only use part of the image or resize.

Then start conversion

The converted file should be found at the bottom of your screen. If not, look in your download files folder.

It is now ready to be uploaded into Design Space as a SVG file.

Other online options include:

www.autotracer.org

www.picsvg.com

www.svgconvertor .com

www.pngtosvg.com

There are a bunch of sites that will convert a JPG or PNG to a SVG. Just do a search for convert to svg, photo to svg or image converter to find them. The quality of the conversion will vary from site to site so experiment to find the one that works best for you.

Turning photos into SVG files

This allows you to turn photos into images that can be used on decals, vinyl, cloth, wood, stencils, card stock or any other material you choose.

Be sure to select an image that has good light and dark contrast.

Then go to this site:

https://online.rapidresizer.com/photograph-to-pattern.php

You'll have an option to make the images darker or lighter. There is also an adjustment to make the lines sharper or softer. There are several other options you can use to change the appearance of the image.

When you're done you can now save it to your computer, then upload into Design Space to make further edits.

SVG files may not always appear as you want when you first upload.

You may need to do some editing to get the files to look exactly how you want. There are options in Design Space to make some changes, but for advanced edits you may need to work with one of the software options we'll talk about later in this chapter.

Why design custom images

The first reason is because you simply can't find what you're looking for. You have an image in mind that you want for your project and you just can't locate what you want. Not in the form you imagine it, anyway. So you'll need to create it.

If you're an artist, you may want to draw your own images to use in your Cricut projects. But you don't have to do this to create your own images. You can start with an image file and make changes.

Another reason is if you want to sell the projects you make. Many images you'll find online are of popular Disney characters for example. While you can usually get away with using these for crafts for your personal use, you can not put trademarked images on items you want to sell. Even when you purchase the images, they will say for personal use only, not for commercial use. If you want to use the images for items you're selling, contact the seller and ask the cost of a commercial license. Just because an image can be found in Google images does not mean it's free from copyright restrictions.

And still another reason is you want to create a passive income stream where you design files and sell them over and over again.

Software Apps or websites for creating and editing SVG files

There are several software options for working with SVG files to use with your Cricut. You may have to try a few to find out which one suits your specific needs and wants.

Personally, I find it easier to work with design software on my computer but some are available for iPads and IPhones and I know crafters who find that works better for them. It may be more convenient if you do a lot of your work away from home.

Design Space – This is the software specifically created for working with Cricut machines. All Explore models as well as the Cricut Maker, Cricut Joy and any new machines the Provo Craft company design will probably work with it as well. If you use other software to edit images, you will eventually upload them into Design Space before you can cut them. This software is available for free.

Adobe Illustrator – This software is one of the best in the industry. It has a wide variety of tools you can use to work with many types of images, including SVG files. It has a 7 day free trial but will have to be purchased after that. It will take some time to learn but it can create intricate patterns. Because it's so popular you can find many videos and guides online to help with your learning curve. (There is also a SVG Kit plugin that enables Photoshop, Photoshop Elements and InDesign to work with SVG files.)

With Illustrator you can draw your own designs and turn them into SVG files. This is perfect for an artist who wants to create their own unique images.

Inkscape – This is a popular software for working with SVG files. And since it's open source software there is no cost. (They hope you'll make a small donation.) You can upload PNG or JPG files, layer the colors, and then save as a SVG file. You can create SVG files from raster and other images as well.

Make the Cut – (MTC) Is easy to learn but also includes advanced editing tools. Works with many types of images including SVG's. The interface is user friendly and makes it easy to convert other types of files into SVG files. This software is available for a price.

Sure Cuts a Lot – (SCAL) This is one of the most popular third party software options used by Cricut users. A big advantage is it allows user to draw their own artwork using simple tools. It also has advanced features for editing such as grouping, layering, and welding together images and text. You can use the trace feature to turn raster images into a SVG. It's also a paid option.

Gimp – Is another open source software which costs nothing but a voluntary donation. It is similar to Adobe and has a learning curve. But for a free option it may be worth the effort to learn how to use the tools. Older versions were not SVG compatible, I'm glad they made the improvement.

If you're looking for free vector editing software that you do not have to download and install there are online options.

Vectr – Free graphics software used to create vector graphics online. www.vectr.com

Photopea – An advanced image editor, which works with both raster and vector graphics. Use it for simple tasks like resizing images or create designs online from scratch. www.photopea.com

There are paid versions as well.

Vector Magic – Easily convert images to vectors with real full-color tracing. www.vectormagic.com

Vectorizer – Convert raster images to scalable vector graphics with a three day free trial. www.vectorizer.io

How to do a reverse image search

Have you ever seen a quote on a coffee cup or a cute image on a t-shirt and wished you could find that same SVG file? Well now you can. If the file is available online just do a reverse image search in Google to find it.

Take a screenshot of just the design and save it. Go to www.images.google.com Click on the camera to search by image.

Then click Upload an image and Browse for the picture you want to find and click on it.

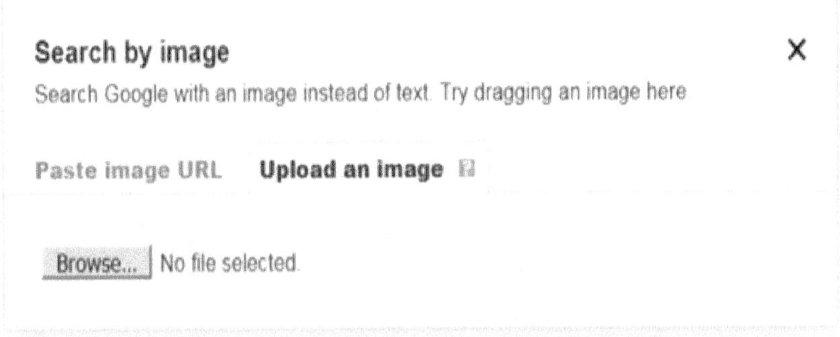

Finally hit Search by image to get these results.

With this tip you now have a way to find that perfect image for any Cricut project.

Combine SVG images with photos

SGV images work well by themselves but don't forget you can add embellishments like you do with scrapbook pages or combine a SVG with a photograph. Add frames, borders, or corners to photographs to really make them pop before transferring them to glass, ceramics, wood, mirror or cloth.

Dress up existing art work

Do you like to draw or color? The relaxing effect coloring has on us has fueled the adult coloring craze. Why not add a SVG border to your artwork before framing.

If you want to know what else to do with finished coloring pages check out Coloring Crafts. Besides product recommendations and advanced coloring techniques it's filled with craft projects for both kids and adults.

Chapter Four - Troubleshooting SVG Files

Like everything else worth doing, working with your Cricut using SVG files requires a learning curve. You may experience some problems along the way. I encourage you not to give up. Remember what it felt like the first time you tried weeding an intricate vinyl pattern? You probably ripped some of it up and maybe eventually trashed it.

TIP: Go to custom settings and use the Washi tape setting when cutting small or intricate cuts to get better results. You may have to add more pressure when working with vinyl.

But then, the next time you did better. You learned that patience works wonders with those types of tasks. If you get in a hurry or let yourself get anxious, it's much harder to achieve the desired result. So be patient with yourself and try to enjoy the process, not just the end result.

One of the best ways to avoid frustration is to start with basic files with only two or three layers of color that are not overly intricate. You'll be able to build your confidence working with these files. When you start with complex images it's easy to get discouraged.

TIP: When cutting complex images with many design elements try using the **Attach** or **Weld** option in Design Space to make it easier to work with.

In the resource section I list Facebook groups for Cricut users. There are always people in the group who are available to answer questions. Search for free SVG files to find other groups there are a bunch of them.

Tips and tricks for creating or working with SVG files

Simple images will upload into Design Space ready to go but more complex files will need some editing before they are ready to use.

After you upload the image onto your canvas, look on the right side of your screen to see the **Layers** panel of your image. It will show a thumbnail of each layer, the color of the layer, and the cut attribute such as score layer, cut layer, or draw layer, etc. If the layer is visible there will be an eye icon on the far right.

Working with files with score lines

The images will all show as cut files, (this is the default) but you'll need to change some to score lines. The score lines are to show you where the project is to be folded after the project has been cut, but they should not be cut. The score lines will just be a line in your thumbnail, there will be no color. To make the change, click on the layer you want to change and then go to **Linetype** on the upper left of your screen. There is a dropdown menu that says, **Cut**, **Draw**, **Score**. Click on the **Score** option. Score lines will now be shown as dotted lines instead of solid.

You can also change the color of each layer by using the color box option at the top left of the canvas. This lets you play around with different color choices now you see what the project will look like when completed. You can use any color of material for each layer when you make your cuts.

To ungroup the layers, click on the **UnGroup** icon on the top right of your screen. Right clicking on the object also brings up a popup window with many options.

You'll then need to attach layers that must stay together. These are the layers that must be cut or scored at the same time. Click on the layers and then click on **Attach** at the bottom right of your screen. You can now move each layer around on the canvas and the cut and score lines will stay with their correct layer.

If you aren't able to use the **Attach** function go back and make sure you've ungrouped everything. When all the layers are ungrouped, you shouldn't have a problem attaching any layers. There can be more than one group in each project and they will all need to be ungrouped before you can work with them.

You can arrange which layers are on top (visible) using the **Arrange** button at the top of the screen. This will not affect how they are cut, it just makes easier to see what the project looks like on the screen.

After you're done, be sure and save your project. If you decide to make changes, SAVE AGAIN!

Remember, you can always undo any change by hitting the **Undo** icon on the upper left of your screen. Or you can click Control Z for PC or Command Z on a Mac. This comes in handy when you click the wrong thing or change your mind.

Problems uploading SVG's to Cricut Design Space

If you're trying to upload a zip file you'll get an error message. You need to unzip/extract the files and then upload the specific file/image you want. You can't import the compressed zipped file.

When your file opens up in your web browser it means you tried to open it by double clicking. You need to import and then upload instead.

When you get a message saying "Your file contains unsupported items" it could mean several things.

The first is you may have editable text in the file. You will need to change the text to a shape in Adobe Illustrator or another program.

The file may contain pattern fills. This means the image has shadows, gradient colors, photos, textures, or anything that keeps the file from allowing colors to be layered. You export the file as a JPG or PNG then upload into Design Space. It will not be layered like a SVG file but you can use the print and cut feature at least.

Clipping paths are another potential problem. They blur colors together so there's no clear separation. You can flatten the image using tools in Adobe Illustrator or use the print and cut feature.

There may be linked images in the file. This means there's a link that takes you to another site instead of the image actually being in the file. You'll need to download or embed the image into the file.

All of the above can be corrected by working with the files in Inkscape or Adobe Illustrator before trying to upload into Design Space.

TIP: If you get a Remove Exclusive Content warning log out of Design Space and close the new desktop App. If it persists clear your cache (temporary internet files) and try again.

Avoid scattered elements all over the mat

When the image you're using contains words and you want to cut them all out of the same color make sure the design is grouped on the mat and click **Attach** before you **Make It**.

If the words are different colors just **Group** each color together, then **Group** the whole design and click **Attach**.

Uploaded image not showing on the canvas

The image has been inserted on the canvas but you can't see it, what happened? Some files import so large you don't see them on the screen. When that happens look at the top tool bar for **Size** and **Position**. Change the size to something smaller and scroll down until you see the image drag it to where you want. Or change both positions to zero and it will pop up to the left corner of the canvas.

SVG viewers

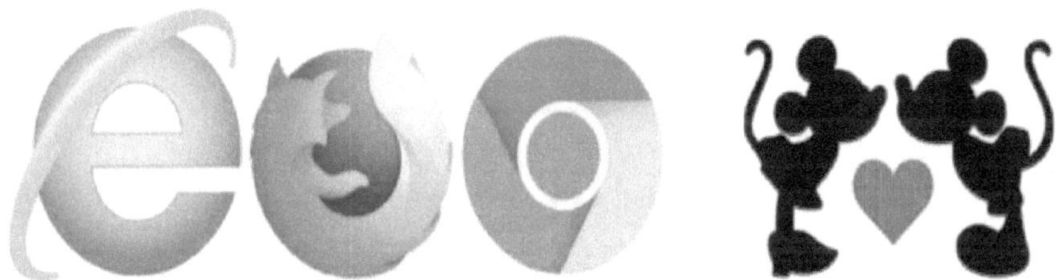

Since Windows associates a browser icon with SVG files instead of generating a thumbnail picture to show what the image looks like, poses a problem. You have to double click it to open it in the browser to view it which is annoying. That's where Apps, add-ons, plugins and extensions come in.

They provide a picture of a SVG file. You can install software or do a search to see what is available for your particular browser.

There are several options like File Viewer Plus, SVG Viewer, Free SVG Viewer and SVG viewer extension for Windows Explorer. To see it in action go to the Video Tutorial chapter.

Visit the Chrome web store and search for SVG to find extensions. Click on More extensions to bring up what's available from SVG grabbers to converters.

TIP: If you don't want to install a SVG viewer here's a workaround. Copy the JPG file that comes with the SVG into a folder called SVG Database. That way you know the name of the file and what the SVG looks like.

SVG fonts VS installable fonts

I'm here to save you the heartache of buying a SVG font and then trying to install it like you do other fonts to use in Design Space. I know I told you that SVGS are the best files for crafters so why can't you use SVG fonts? They won't work and here's why.

A SVG font differs from a regular installable font in that it's used for web design **not cutting machines**. They contain multiple colors, transparencies, textures and gradients which make them unreadable in Design Space.

They will not appear on the canvas when you type them on a keyboard. Do not confuse these with an individual alphabet cut file that designers draw and save in the SVG format.

Here's an example of what I mean. The designer goes through the entire alphabet drawing each individual letter and saves it as a cut file named A.svg, B.svg, C.svg etc. and sells them on Etsy. These letters are like other image files that can be uploaded into Design Space and inserted into a project.

Just think of **SVG fonts as images** and not letters on a keyboard.

Design Space comes with some free fonts but you may want to install more system fonts on your computer to make them available for crafting.

When choosing a font that will cut well look for ones with smooth edges. Remember when working with vinyl bold fonts are easier to weed than thin, fancy ones with of lot of swirls.

TIP: Can't find the new font you just installed? Hit the refresh button if that doesn't do it try logging off or closing Design Space give it a minute and search again, it should show up now.

Chapter Five - Some Money Making Ideas

Making money with your crafts is not as hard as you might think. First decide whether you want to start a small business or you just want your hobby to pay for itself. Do you want to sell physical products or just digital ones?

Before starting your craft business decide if you want to sell offline, online or both. Do you want to sell from your own website, sell from an Etsy shop, Facebook page or YouTube channel? The more you know about your business needs the easier it will be to reach your goals.

Several of the websites mentioned in this book are marketplaces where you can sell the SVG files you create. They also have an affiliate program where you get paid when you send them a paying customer.

Merch by Amazon is an opportunity for all you t-shirt designers to reach millions of customers worldwide with no upfront investment or cost.

Develop your skills as a freelancer and offer your design skills to others. Designing mock ups for other online sellers who need them to sell their cut files and products could be an opportunity worth investigating

Become a blogger for hire. Create a craft project using one of their free SVG files complete with pictures and step by step instructions. Contact the blog owner and offer to sell them your information. Website owners need fresh content to keep their visitors coming back.

Running a profitable website requires a lot of skills like site maintenance, advertising, social media posting, email list management and on and on leaving little time for designing. Contact blog owners and offer to design cut files for them. Who knows it may lead to a successful partnership.

Businesses use promotional items to advertise and generate customer loyalty. Contact a local business and offer to create a custom design they can use on the next promotional campaign.

If you enjoy teaching others why not create a course showing other crafters how to design SVG files.

Print on demand (POD)

There are a ton of sites online where designers can make money using print on demand technology. You just add your SVG design to any number of items, like clothes, coffee cups, wall art, stationery, personalized gifts and just about any other product you can imagine.

When your customer buys the item the POD site ships it to them and you share the profits.

Some print on demand companies include zazzle.com, society6.com and redbubble.com to mention a few.

These are just a few ways you can turn your love of creating beautiful designs into cold hard cash.

T-Shirt decorating on steroids

As a Cricut crafter you probably have done your fair share of vinyl projects. If you're tired of decorating the same old things then check out my 130 craft vinyl ideas book filled with tips, tricks and troubleshooting techniques plus money making ideas galore.

If you want to take t-shirt decorating to the next level why not give sublimation transfer a try. It differs from heat transfer vinyl (HTV) in that is uses ink that becomes part of the fabric instead of just sitting on top. It doesn't crack, peel, or wash off. It lasts longer and feels softer. The only drawback is it only works on white or light colored fabrics.

All you need is sublimation transfer paper, an Epson ink jet printer, refillable cartridges, sublimation ink and a home oven.

Sublimation also works on coffee cups but requires a mug press machine.

TIP: Remember, when working with iron on vinyl you'll need to "mirror" the image. It will look backwards but be correct when you iron it on to the fabric.

Cricut Infusible Ink for sublimation

If you don't want to convert a printer with sublimation ink Cricut has their own pre-printed Infusible Ink transfer sheets in solid colors and patterns as well as Infusible Ink pens and markers for sublimation.

They also provide blank items like t-shirts, coasters, tote bags and onesies to apply the designs too.

Just use Design Space and an EasyPress or another heat press which heats up to 400 degrees Fahrenheit for best results. With Infusible Ink you don't have to use a mug press for coffee cups a home oven works fine.

Chapter Six - Where to Find Free SVG Files

Some of these sites you may be familiar with while others will be an exciting find. These websites are filled with beautiful and unique cutting files just waiting for you to download. Have fun!

100 Directions
https://www.100directions.com/creativity/create-with-cricut/svg-cutting-files/
Share ideas that will inspire happy moments and creative mojo.

17turtles
http://www.17turtles.com/p/digital-cut-files.htm
Juliana offers inspiration, tips, tutorials, sketches, and free digital cut files.

A Girl and a Glue Gun
https://www.agirlandagluegun.com/category/cut-file
These are Kimbo's free files for fast, easy and cute crafts.

Albion Gould
https://www.albiongould.com/?s=free+svg
Traditional crafts with a quirky, modern edge and a little geek culture thrown in.

Apexemb Designs
https://apexembdesigns.com/cuttables/subject/all?keys=&commerce_price_amount=1&field_font_type_tid=All
A family run business specializing in cuttable SVG designs.

Artsy Fartsy Mama
https://www.artsyfartsymama.com/search?q=free+svg
Free printables and SVG cut files.

Bird's Cards
https://www.birdscards.com/free-svg-cut-files/
Provides easy to complete SVG projects besides cards and envelopes.

Black Cats SVG
https://www.blackcatssvg.com/collections/free-files
Here you can enjoy a nice collection of SVG files from several different

categories for both personal and commercial use.

Brooklyn Berry Designs
https://brooklynberrydesigns.com/category/crafts/svg-files/
An interior designer helps you create DIY projects.

Bundle SVG
https://bundlesvg.com/product-category/free-svg-files/
They provide free resources for your crafting needs in these file formats
SVG, PNG, EPS and DXF

Burton Avenue
https://burtonavenue.com/category/free_svg_files_for_silhouette_cricut/
Angie welcomes you to her free files page where you can create your own
DIY projects using your electronic cutter.

By Dawn Nichole
https://bydawnnicole.com/category/creative-arts/free-svg-cut-files/
Dawn has products and resources for busy creatives who want to learn, enjoy
and de-stress.

Caluya Design
https://caluyadesign.com/freebie-gallery/
All of Saori's free SVGs are made from scratch with love.

Chicgetti
https://chicfetti.com/file-category/free-svg-files/
Jenny's website is dedicated to sharing creative & chic ideas that will inspire
you to create something today.

Craftables
https://shopcraftables.com/free-svg-cut-files/
Craftables sells vinyl and has a bunch of free cut files in a variety of
categories.

Craft Bundles
https://craftbundles.com/product-category/free-svg-cut-files/
They have a variety of designs for all your craft projects and offer a
commercial license.

Craft House SVG
https://crafthousesvg.com/collections/freebies
You are allowed to use their designs on physical end products and digital printable files for sale.

Craft N Cuts
https://craftncuts.com/product-category/freebies/
These freebies come with a lifetime commercial license.

Crafting for Business
https://cuttingforbusiness.com/category/free-cut-files/
Besides free files they offer advice on starting your own cutting business.

Craft With Sarah
https://www.craftwithsarah.com/product-category/free-svgs-for-cricut/
Sarah is a Cricut crafter and card maker from the UK that designs layered mandala patterns.

Creative Fabrica
https://www.creativefabrica.com/freebies/free-crafts/
Free SVG files for crafters complete with commercial license.

Creative Market
https://creativemarket.com/free-goods
Free goods of the week can be vectors, clipart, fonts, SVG cut files and more.

Creativity in Chaos
https://www.creativityinchaos.com/svg-library
Stephanie has a bunch of SVG bow templates.

Crunchy Pickle
https://www.crunchypickle.com/product-category/free-svg-cut-files/
Cissy's designs are created with the smallest amount of edit nodes possible to give you a super smooth and cleaner cut that cuts faster.

Cute Crafting
https://www.cutecrafting.com/svg-cutting-files/
Kristi likes designing SVG files that her visitors will enjoy.

Cut That Design

https://cutthatdesign.com/
Free cutting files for personal use, with the opportunity of purchasing commercial use rights.

Daydream into Reality
https://www.daydreamintoreality.com/printables-library/
Catalina says she is creating the most beautiful and helpful printables library that the Internet has ever seen!

Design Bundles
https://designbundles.net/free-design-resources
Free SVG's, graphic packs, illustrations, icons, templates, backgrounds, textures and more.

Designer Printables
https://designerprintables.com/printables/free-svg-cut-files/
A resource for premium graphics, illustrations and crafting cut files.

Designs By Miss Mandee
https://www.designsbymissmandee.com/tag/free-svg/
Mandee is a professional graphic designer who shares her designs helping people to fulfill their creative dreams.

Designs by Winther
https://designsbywinther.com/category/free-svg-files/
Completely free cut files by Louise for all your creative projects for personal use.

Digitalist Designs
https://www.digitalistdesigns.com/freebies/
Falyn is an illustrator that offers her creations to crafters who love cut files.

Digitanza
https://digitanza.com/product-category/free/
This is a marketplace for craters and designers.

Domestic Heights
https://domesticheights.com/free-svg-cut-files-bundles/
Ilyssa has hundreds of SVG cut files in her resource library that are all free.

Dreaming Tree
https://www.3dsvg.com/product-category/free-svg-files/?orderby=date
They have an APP to tell you when new freebies are added plus videos
showing how to assemble the project. Very cool!

Easy Cuts It
https://easycutsit.com/product-category/freebies/
This site is dedicated to the creation of SVG files as digital downloads.

Elena Maria Designs
https://elenamariadesigns.com/collections/free-svg-files-1
Professional SVG files for Cricut & Silhouette crafters.

Everyday Party Magazine
https://everydaypartymag.com/?s=free+svg
Celebrating your everyday moments using SVG images.

Flavors Store
https://flavoursstore.com/collections/freebie
They share digital clip art, printables, cutting files for scrapbooks, cards, T-
shirts or other crafting projects but only for personal use.

Free Cut Files
https://freecutfiles.com/svg-free/
The sight was started by four girls who offer free SVG cut files, inspiration,
DIY creations, and font suggestions.

Free Pik
https://www.freepik.com/popular-vectors
This site has free images in several formats like photos, vectors, PSD and AI
that can be converted to SVG's or used as is.

Free Pretty Things for You
https://www.freeprettythingsforyou.com/category/free-cut-files-svg/
Beautiful digital papers, graphics, printables, and SVG design files.

The Free SVG Blog
https://freesvgs.blogspot.com/
Download free vector files for your scrapbooking, card making, stamping,
vinyl decor, paper crafting and more.

Free SVG Designs
https://freesvgdesigns.com/
Erin's site is a creative resource for you to find free cut files and monogram
fonts.

Free SVGs
https://freesvgs.com/
Tiffany is a self-taught artist that enjoys making cut files.

Frog Prince Paperie
https://frogprincepaperie.com/?s=free+svg
Paula offers craft projects as well as a few lifestyle hacks.

FunLurn SVG
https://funlurnsvg.com/product-category/free-svg-cut-files/
Ruchira serves crafters who run small business by designing craft files for
them.

Get Silvered
http://www.getsilvered.com/freebie-svg-files/
Pam makes cut files and loves to give them to her readers.

Gina C. Creates
https://ginaccreates.com/category/svgcutfiles/
On this site you will find hand-drawn and hand-lettering vector designs.

Gjs Art
https://gjsart.com/category/free-svg-files/
Their SVG graphics are high quality vector art that can be used in most
commercial projects.

Glitter Bomb Creative
https://www.glitterbombcreative.com/category/svg-cut-files/
The site is for people looking for creative files from graphic designers with
craft and printing backgrounds who love everything free.

Happiness is Homemade
https://www.happinessishomemade.net/category/svg/
Heidi features crafts, DIY projects, home decor, SVG's and lots of printables.

Happy Go Lucky
https://www.happygoluckyblog.com/category/svg-cut-file/
Kara wants you to enjoy her fun and inexpensive DIY projects.

Happy Crafters
https://www.happycrafters.com/free-svg-cut-file-share-free-spring-cut-files-for-cricut-and-silhouette
Elisha's motto is don't worry be crafty because creativity makes the world a much better place.

Hela Crafty
https://helacrafty.com/
Browse and download any of Helena's SVG's from her freebie gallery.

Hello Creative Family
https://hellocreativefamily.com/category/svg-files/
Crystal ignites your creative passion to live the handmade lifestyle.

Hello SVG
https://hellosvg.com/
Commercial licenses are included in your free downloads.

Hey, Let's Make Stuff
https://heyletsmakestuff.com/?s=free
Cori's blog has easy crafts, fun printables, and SVG files for cutting on your Cricut machine.

HoopMama Designs
https://hoopmama.com/product-category/freebies/
Jeanna's motto is crafting is more than a hobby. Besides free files her embroidery files are cuttable as well.

iheart SVG
https://iheartsvg.com/
Francesca makes her own cutables and posts them for us all.

I Should Be Mopping the Floor
https://www.ishouldbemoppingthefloor.com/p/free-svg-files.html
Commercial licensing is available on some of Kristie's free SVG files.

Jennie Masterson
https://jenniemasterson.com/category/free-svgs/
Jennie creates patterns and projects that are clear and easy to follow. Her sewing designs might be what you Cricut Maker users are looking for.

Jennifer Maker
https://jennifermaker.com/?s=free+svg
Jennifer is your crafty friend that helps you with an endless list of craft projects.

Jonas Stensgaard
https://www.jonasstensgaard.com/free-craft-files-svgs-and-more
Jonas is a graphic designer that continues to explore his creative nature.

Kabram Krafts
http://kabramkrafts.com/svg-library/
Kristin enjoys creating new files for cutting machines and even takes request for any shapes you need.

Kayla Makes
https://kaylamakes.com/free-downloads/
Kayla calls herself occasionally crafty and shares her DIY ideas.

Kelly Leigh Creates
https://kellyleighcreates.com/?s=free+sg
Kelly's mission is to inspire you through hand lettering, cut files, and graphic design tutorials.

Kimber Dawn
https://kimberdawnco.com/category/free-cut-files/
Run by two friends whose mission is to be your ultimate creative business resource.

Koti Beth
https://www.kotibeth.com/search/label/svg
Cari really likes adding bling to her projects with glitter and says she'll put vinyl on anything that sits still long enough.

Leap of Faith Crafting
https://leapoffaithcrafting.com/free-svg-files/

Amy wants to help everyone along their crafting journey.

Lemony Fizz
https://shop.lemonyfizz.com/collections/svg-files
Rhoda designs SVG files to use with her Cricut, digital printables, as well as crafty paper projects, and shares them all with all of us.

Lemon Thistle
https://www.lemonthistle.com/?s=free+svg
Colleen believes having beautiful things doesn't mean spending a lot of money just use a little creativity.

Life Sew Savory
https://lifesewsavory.com/tag/scan-n-cut/
Emily has a huge resource of free craft SVG files including sewing projects that you Cricut Maker users can adapt.

Little Scraps of Heaven Designs
https://www.littlescrapsofheavendesigns.com/pages/free-file.htm
Tricia creates premade layouts and paper piecings. She loves to see little works of art come to life.

Little Stuff
https://www.littlestuff.me/free-digital-cut-files/
Tina has designed quite a few cut files from scratch and wants to share her freebies.

Liz on Call
https://lizoncall.com/tag/free-cut-file/
Liz is a creator of beautiful things like cut files to decorate t-shirts, mugs, totes, home decor and more.

Love SVG
https://lovesvg.com/free-svg-cut-files/
Over 9000 free SVG cut files some with commercial license.

Love the Day
https://love-the-day.com/svgs
Lindi organizes parties in unique and creative ways while creating printable designs for your entertaining inspiration.

Love Paper Crafts
https://www.lovepapercrafts.com/category/freebies/svg/
Chelsea provides free and premium printable and cuttable files to crafters and do-it-yourself divas.

Lukasz Adam
https://lukaszadam.com/illustrations
Lukasz is the free illustration guy that has vector illustrations for commercial and personal use for everyone.

Mad In Crafts
https://madincrafts.com/free-svg-file-downloads/
Jessica has no art background, and all her DIY skills are learned from her dad or YouTube.

Maggie Rose Design Co
https://maggierosedesignco.com/product-category/free-svg-cut-files/
Maggie will help you make amazing creations even if you're not an artist or have the "creative gene".

Main Road Digital Creations
https://mainroaddigitalcreations.com/
Tracy shares many years of crafting experiences with all of us and lots of digital designs too.

Mighty Mamma
https://mightymamma.com/mighty-mammas-weekly-free-svg-files/
Trina finds sharing especially gratifying and wants to see photos of what you make using her cut files.

Miss Kate Cuttables
https://www.misskatecuttables.com/products/free-stuff/
Offers the craft community the highest quality SVG files, best fonts, cute designs, and of course freebies.

Monica's Creative Room
https://monicascreativeroom.se/
Click on categories to find all her cutting files in these formats. DFX, PDF, SVG, WPC, Studio, JPG and MTC.

Morgan Day Designs
https://morgandaydesigns.com/collections/free-svg-files
Pamela also offers resources and support to help craft businesses like yours
grow.

My Designs in the Chaos
https://mydesignsinthechaos.com/?s=cut+files
Michelle is the creative director behind her easy to use cut files.

Nap Time Alternative
https://naptimealt.com/introducing-freebie-library/
Kathryn offer free files to go along with tutorials in her Free Resource
Library.

Paper Issues
https://paperissuesstore.myshopify.com/collections/free-files
This site has a large design team offering a ton of SVG files.

Pattern Revolution
https://www.patternrevolution.com/graphics
They're a collective of women focused on encouraging and educating the
modern sewing enthusiast by providing instant digital downloads.

Perfectly Stylish Cuts
https://www.perfectstylishcuts.com/category/freebies/
Idalia has a cut file design library full of free SVG files.

Persia Lou
https://persialou.com/cut-files/
Alexis shares her creative, crafty, fun with all of us and of course SVG's.

Pineapple Paper Co
https://pineapplepaperco.com/category/free-downloads/free-svg-files/
Charynn is excited to share her SVG files, printables, and craft projects with
artisans.

Pixlr
https://pixlr.com/stock/freebies/all/
Enables everyone to create, edit and share images online with ease.

Polka Dot Chair
https://www.polkadotchair.com/?s=svg
Melissa finds joy in creating arts and crafts with her happy cut files.

Poofy Cheeks
http://poofycheeks.com/tag/free-svg/
Kelsey is a graphic designer and blogger with free SVG's.

Practically Functional
https://www.practicallyfunctional.com/?s=free+svg
Jess provides crafts and DIY projects for all skill levels.

Printable Crush
https://printablecrush.com/category/free-printables/svg-files/
Erin encourages you to learn how to design some printables yourself.

Printable Cuttable Creatables
https://www.printablecuttablecreatables.com/product-category/freebies/
Kristin specializes in hand drawn, high quality SVG files and digital patterns
that are easy to cut and assemble.

Ready2cut
https://ready2cut.com/product-category/free/
These designs are intended for personal and commercial use.

Red Earth and Gum Trees
https://www.redearthandgumtrees.com/free-svg-files.html
Free vectorized files to create beautiful, personalized gifts for you, your
home, family, and friends.

Repurposing Junkie
https://repurposingjunkie.com/?s=free+svg
Keri hopes her website is inspiring and helpful when you repurpose stuff
using her cut files for Cricut and other cutters.

Ruffles and Rain Boots
https://rufflesandrainboots.com/free-svgs/
Sarah is a creative gal that serves up SVG files and tutorials for easy crafts.

Savana's Design

https://savanasdesign.com/freebies/
Savana designs free SVG files for your Cricut cutter.

Scarlett Rose Designs
https://scarlettrosedesigns.com/collections/free-svg-files
All designs come with a small business commercial license.

See Lindsay
https://seelindsay.com/category/svg-files-printables/svg-files/
Lindsay loves her Cricut and likes to create easy, inexpensive projects with
free SVG files.

Sherry K Designs
https://sherykdesigns.com/product-category/freebies/
I like her card making kits and party favor gift boxes.

Shirley's Cards
https://shirleystemplates.blogspot.com/
Shirley designs free card templates and toppers as cut files.

Shop Craftables
https://shopcraftables.com/free-svg-cut-files/
Craftables started as a decal business and recommends vinyl products.

Silhouette Design Store
https://www.silhouettedesignstore.com/designs?free_designs=1
Cricut users make sure you select SVG before downloading your free files.

Simply Crafty SVGS
https://www.simplycraftysvgs.com/product-category/freebies/
Sandy's selection of free vectors includes gift boxes, cards and even 3D
designs.

So Fontsy
https://sofontsy.com/collections/free
These freebies always include the commercial use license.

Special Heart Studio
https://specialheartstudio.com/product-category/freebies/
Gjoa is a fellow crafter who hopes her designs inspire you.

Specialty Materials
https://specialtymaterials.com/free-cut-files/
They provide digitally printable media for textile decoration and offer free HTV (heat transfer vinyl) samples.

Sun Catcher Studio
https://suncatcherstudio.com/patterns/cricut-designs/
Jodie and Bill enjoy teaching others how to make handmade items.

SVG and Me
https://svgandme.com/start-here/
Get access to their Free SVG Library when you sign-up.

SVG Cuts
http://svgcuts.com/blog/free-designs/
Mary is the artist behind all the designs you see and is an award winner from Martha Stewart.

SVG Cutable Files
https://svgcuttablefiles.com/collections/freebies
Jennifer has cut files and designs that are easy to customize.

SVG Cut Studio
https://svgcutstudio.com/collections/free-svg-files
The designs they create are for crafters who want to make gifts, DIY projects, scrapbooks and screen-prints.

SVG Cutting Files
http://svgcuttingfiles.com/catalog.php?category=1
Paper crafting made easy with the help of their design team.

SVF Files Free
https://svgfilesfree.com/?s=free+svg
Use your Cricut machine to make amazing creations with Jane's designs.

SVG Font Market
https://svgfontmarket.com/collections/freebies
A marketplace for designers that provide creative and original designs including free ones.

SVG Designs
https://www.svgdesigns.com/list/svg/freesvgdesigns
Their mission is to provide crafters a unique outlet where they can both shop and find inspiration for their next SVG project.

SVG Files Free
https://svgfilesfree.com/page/2/
Jane showcases her designs with free cut files.

SVG For Cricut
https://www.svgforcricut.com/product-category/free-svg-downloads
At SVG For Cricut they ar committed to bringing you high quality, craft-friendly products, and free files complete with commercial licenses.

Sweet Red Poppy
https://sweetredpoppy.com/category/cricut-2/free-svg-files/
Kimberly is obsessed with all things Cricut, sewing and crafting.

Swing Design
https://www.swingdesign.com/pages/free-design-files
You can download 200 designs in zipped files or individually.

That's What Che Said
https://www.thatswhatchesaid.net/category/freebies/free-svg/
These free cut files are SVG and DXF files that can be used with an electronic cutting machine like Cricut or Silhouette.

The Country Chic Cottage
https://www.thecountrychiccottage.net/?s=free+svg
Angie shares Cricut tutorials and crafts with all of you.

Tauni Everett
https://taunieverett.com/?s=free+svg
Tauni has cut files for craft projects for adults and kids.

The Craft Patch Blog
https://www.thecraftpatchblog.com/?s=free+svg
Turn your hobby into something more with these creative ideas.

The Crazy Craft Lady

https://thecrazycraftlady.com/?s=free+svg
Aimee has DIY projects plus seasonal decor cut files, and craft ideas.

The Design Hippo
https://thedesignhippo.com/category/svg-cut-files/
Neema and hubby Vijay are fascinated by design, color, technology, and all things DIY which includes free vectorized images.

The Girl Creative
https://www.thegirlcreative.com/product-category/svg/
Free cut files amongst the paid ones so look around.

The Kingston Home
https://thekingstonhome.com/blog/category/svg-printables/
Beth thinks she's the luckiest girl in the world because she gets to play with paper and glue for a living.

The Navage Patch
https://www.thenavagepatch.com/?s=free+svg
Handan and Greg offer cut files and a printables library.

The Non Crafty Crafter
http://www.thenoncraftycrafter.com/p/my-free-cut-files.html
Narelle likes to pass on what she learns about crafts to her readers.

The Quiet Grove
https://thequietgrove.com/store/free-printables/free-svg-cut-files/
Free SVG and PNG files designed by a husband and wife team.

The Scrap Shoppe
https://www.thescrapshoppeblog.com/?s=free+svg
Michele focuses on creating fun and unique crafts.

The Simply Crafted Life
https://www.thesimplycraftedlife.com/?s=svg
Sarah's designs are for anyone who wants to craft a life that is both creative and simple.

The SVG Stop
https://svgstop.com/freebies

The files are high quality original designs by Shawna. She tests each file to be sure everything works like it supposed to.

Tried & True
https://www.triedandtrueblog.com/?s=free+svg
Vanessa is a life-long crafter who loves creating craft tutorials for projects that are quick, easy, and fun to make.

Unoriginal Mom
https://www.unoriginalmom.com/?submit=Search&s=free+svg+cricut
Meredith provides inspiration, do-able tutorials, and practical ideas for your everyday life.

Vexels
https://www.vexels.com/free-svg-cut-files/
These guys let you download free vector images for your creative projects from a collection of more than 40,000 free vector cut files.

Vintage Glam Studio
https://www.vintageglamstudio.com/?s=svg
This single mom shares her DIY crafts, planner printables, and free SVG designs.

We Can Make That
https://wecanmakethat.me/product-category/free-svg/
Chelly loves designing SVG files to use on crafts and DIY projects.

Where the Smiles Have Been
https://www.wherethesmileshavebeen.com/category/freebies/free-silhouette-cut-files/
Christine has printables and cut files for Silhouette machines but you can still use the SVG version for Cricut machines.

Wunder-Bear Creations
https://wunderbearcreations.com/downloads/category/free-svg-files/
This husband and wife team helps others appreciate & celebrate all the special moments in life.

Chapter Seven - How to Video Tutorials

Seeing it for yourself can make it easier to learn that's why YouTube is such a good teaching tool. You can read about something but when you see it in action all the pieces come together.

Video tutorials are great for learning new stuff, for remembering how to do something you may have forgotten or to find a solution to a nagging problem. I can usually find videos that answer my questions.

It's like having a teacher guiding you each step of the way through your projects. You can work on Design Space from your computer and have a mobile device set up next to it playing the videos you need.

Did you know you can download YouTube videos and watch them offline anytime you want? Just do a search for download YouTube videos if that option appeals to you.

How to avoid an unsupported file error message when uploading an image.
https://youtu.be/GBsTbyx7690

Here's how to fix a corrupt file that won't cut.
https://youtu.be/Vel4Jw1eGkE

Tips for the new desktop Cricut Design Space App.
https://youtu.be/37Ih39VlsU8

SVG viewer extension for Windows Explorer to show thumbnail images.
https://youtu.be/nePIp_LYwAo

Adding free fonts to Design Space and mobile devices.
https://youtu.be/UloP5h6fRmY

These are the free fonts that come with Design Space.
https://youtu.be/LkP4254m_Fc

Use Design Space to make layered SVG files.
https://youtu.be/nk41z4qdY8k

Cleaning up a SVG with the contour button in Design Space.
https://youtu.be/TsJntr87WK0

Create a SVG file in Inkscape.
https://youtu.be/JvntQe8C9qQ

Turn a SVG into a print and cut greeting card.
https://youtu.be/KeyDevwfD4I

Sublimation printing produces vibrant colors on t-shirts.
https://youtu.be/udXr_8sQfg0

Make and sell your own SVG files.
https://youtu.be/8fpIk1PCVMY

Where to sell printables and SVG files.
https://youtu.be/iaChNYmnkLg

Chapter Eight - Helpful FAQ's

I had fun writing this book and I feel it's a helpful, timesaving guide for crafters using any cutting machine that works with SVG files.

I hope you have many years of creative fun with your Cricut, designing beautiful images that can be used on any craft project you can imagine. The answer to these questions will help.

1. Why are SVG files preferable for Cricut? They are created using mathematical points and lines that tell the blade which direction to go. This makes them more suitable for cutting. They are also scalable so you can enlarge or reduce them without losing quality.

2. When I double click on and SVG file it opens in my browser, now what?
When you open a file within a folder your computer uses the appropriate software to open it. Since Windows does not recognize SVG files it uses your browser. You can change this by right clicking on the file, choose Properties and click Change. Then select which application you want to associate with or open SVG files from now on. Windows 10 is a little different. Click on Settings > Apps > Default apps > Set Your Default Programs > Choose default apps by file type scroll down until you see svg or svgz. Click on the Default Program to open a pop up window and choose the new program you want to use. You may have to browse to find it. If you have a lot of files give it time to reset.

3. If I choose to open SVG files by selecting Cricut Design Space as the default program will it open automatically? No. You're just telling your computer which program to associate SVG files with. You'll see the little Cricut icon next to the file name. You will still have to upload the file as usual.

4. Are the free files compatible with the Print and Cut feature in Design Space? Yes, most designers will include high resolution JPG and PNG files in the download folder so you can print and cut the design. Or edit the SVG in Design Space flattening it or changing the **Cut** icon to **Print** in the layers panel.

5. What's a good way to organize cutting files? Separate them by categories and create separate folders for each category or theme. Use sub-folders if you want to get very specific. Keep the ones with a commercial license separate that way you never have to worry about selling anything you make with them.

6. Can I download SVG files on a mobile device from these free sites? Yes and no. Check out their FAQ section to see if there files will download. When using a tablet or phone make sure you have the ability to unzip the files. There are free Apps available to extract the files for both Android an IOS devices.

7. What kinds of files will be included in the download folder? That depends on the designer. They may include some or all of these types which include AI, DXF, EPS, JPEG, JPEG mirrored, PDF, PNG, SVG and a Read Me file.

8. Which cutting machines use SVG files? Practically all cutting machines will work with these files like any Cricut machine that uses Design Space, Silhouette, Pazzles, Brother ScanNCut and Craft Robo, Sizzix Eclips to mention just a few.

9. What special software do I need to read a SVG file? Cricut Design Space, Sure Cuts A Lot (SCAL), Silhouette Design Edition, Make the Cut (MTC), Adobe Illustrator, Inkscape, Corel Draw, Gimp or any other vector design programs that accepts SVG files. It depends on your budget and your needs to decide what's best for you.

10. I downloaded the SVG but I don't see it? Look for a zipped folder or an html file with your browser icon as the thumbnail.

11. Is there an easy way to group a bunch of tiny elements within a design? Hiding layers is a way to simplify the creation process. Use the eye icon in the layers panel to hide the layers you don't want to group. Draw a bounding box around all the pieces you want to group together and hit **Attach**. When you're done just click the eye again to make them reappear.

12. The uploaded SVG looks different it's mostly black and lacks detail. Is the file corrupted? No. Chances are it was designed correctly but Design Space sees the black outline and not a fill color. Do a test cut on scrap paper to see if it cuts the way you expect it to.

13. Can I make money with my Cricut crafts? If you have a commercial license for your images or you draw your own designs, then you can sell your items on sites like Etsy, Amazon, Facebook marketplace, eBay or your own website.

14. Can I use any images that I find online? Many images can be converted from PNG and JPG to a SVG file. The more colors and layers the image has the more complex it will be to work with. You can use files like Disney character pics for personal use, but you cannot sell the items you make using licensed images.

Chapter Nine - Valuable Resources

www.Wordmark.it saves you the trouble of scrolling through all of your installed fonts to find the one that looks the best. Just type in the word or phrase and instantly preview your text in all the fonts on your computer.

Facebook Groups are a great place to get help, share ideas and show off your creations.

Sharing svg's
www.facebook.com/groups/2603516676590745/

Cricut SVG For Beginners
www.facebook.com/groups/3573869589293240/

Free software for creating SVG files. Check out their tutorial section as well.

www.inkscape.org/

www.gimp.org/

Download clipart and free vector images.

www.openclipart.org

www.vectorstock.com/free-vectors

Table of Contents

Introduction
Chapter One - Why Crafters Love SVG Files
Chapter Two - Free SVG Images Online
Chapter Three - Creating Your Own SVG Files
Chapter Four - Troubleshooting SVG Files
Chapter Five - Some Money Making Ideas
Chapter Six - Where to Find Free SVG Files
Chapter Seven - How to Video Tutorials
Chapter Eight - Helpful FAQ's
Chapter Nine - Valuable Resources
About the Author